AF450979

MANGAL MEDIA

Evliya Çelebi Mah. Sadi Konuralp Cad. IKSV Vakfı
No:5 İç Kapı no:2 Beyoğlu / İstanbul
Turkey

Writer
Efe Levent

Artist
Alaa Alhassoun

Book Design
Feyza Daloğlu

Guide to Every City, Efe Levent & Alaa Alhassoun, 2020

ISBN 978-605-70348-0-9

STEVE MCCRACKER PRESENTS

GUIDE TO EVERY CITY

2ND EDITION
with new content!

WRITTEN & ILLUSTRATED BY
EFE LEVENT & ALAA ALHASSOUN

CONTENTS

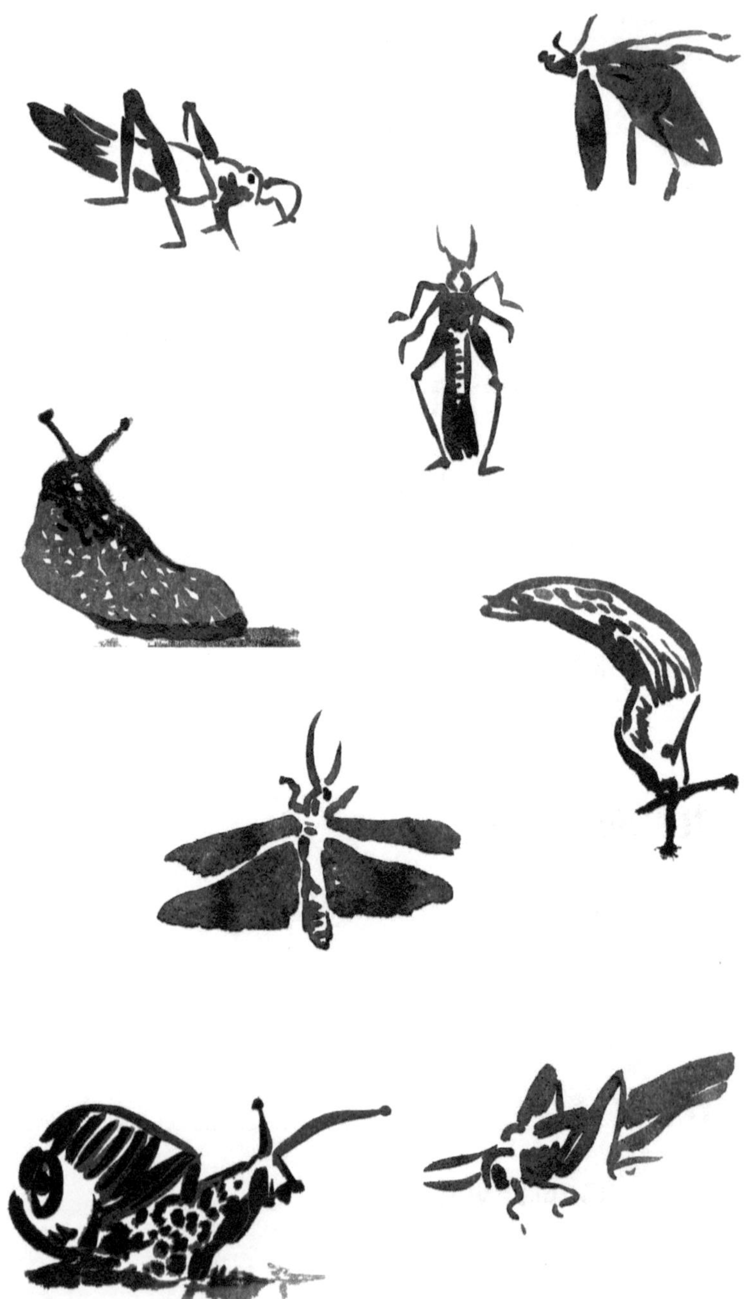

Visitors to Every City are quick to notice that they are standing in a unique and marvellous place. For many centuries, the sights, sounds and the smells of this city have made travellers feel like they have entered a fairyland. Although it has become a cliché, it is hard to get around this fact: Every City is a place *where modernity meets tradition.* There, I said it! Beyond this obvious contrast of old and new, there are also seismic dynamics bubbling below the surface of Every City. These major forces burst out in certain neighbourhoods, each one distinct with their architectural symbolism and their inhabitants.

The Hive is the city's financial and political centre. The afternoon sun splashes a dollop of red across the skyscrapers, as the busy denizens buzz around in a dazzling hurry. This neighbourhood is the home of the "buzzies", who are named after the buzzing sound they make while speeding around in perpetual anxiety. The

Hive is a place where tough decisions are made. Business empires rise and fall within moments. Deals are made and broken over the constant hissing of the city.

The Old Boneyard is the home of the conscientious, hip and creative "hopsters" of Every City. They hop around from cafes to nightclubs, building high-tech incubators over the decaying remnants of industry. As soon as they 'discover' a new place to open up shop they move in unison and swarm down to convert abandoned warehouses into lofts and factories into shared workspaces. These are the innovators of the city, they spot trends from afar and leap onto them, pushing the city forward into the future.

But just because Every City turns it's face to the future, it doesn't mean that it has forgotten the past. Places of worship around Almond Valley still fill up with pious crowds who slither in and out, at a pace which contradicts the dazzling speed of the city. Here is the place where the great masses live, the toiling working classes. Most have immigrated from the landlocked conservative heartlands of the country and are embroiled in their own daily troubles. These are the ordinary citizens of the city. Those who don't have the stamina to withstand the noise of the Hive or the energy to keep up with the ceaseless innovation of the Old Boneyard, slip through the cracks of Every city and end up here to live a modest but quiet life.

—— • ——

THE OLD

BONEYARD

The mystical combination of the past and the future, the hurried rush and the mellow chill are what makes Every City a truly magical place. Just to be clear, Every City is not a tidy Megalopolis with broad avenues that look like they have been drawn with a ruler. It is rather, a sprawling palimpsest of symbols, buildings and roads. It is a juxtaposition of civilisations who salvaged the infrastructure of their predecessors and built upon them. The conflict is far from over. The residents of Every City are locked in a perpetual deadlock, a cultural cold war to answer a simple question: "who owns Every City?"

I am startled when famous author Maji Homsin asks me this question rhetorically as we are drinking tea on the Purple Tower, overlooking the Old Boneyard. The generous early afternoon sun warms our femurs. We are overlooking the banks of Every City Bay where factories and warehouses sprung like mushrooms during the age of industrialisation. With the massive growth of creative industries, these red brick buildings have been cleaned from their layers of soot and gradually changed hands. Instead of housing furniture manufacturers and textile mills, they are now hosting cool hip advertising agencies and international art galleries. Homsin is one of the pioneers who first settled in the Old Boneyard. His hand gently hovers over the landscape like an affectionate

THE OLD BONEYARD

grandfather who remembers "when all this was fields".

The Purple Tower is an appropriate place to meet, it truly captures the essence of the Old Boneyard. The tower was built a hundred years ago by a modernising but despotic ruler. The idea for a tower was first suggested by foreign emissaries as a means of bribing this fiercely nationalist ruler to become more pliant to their demands. The original suggestion was to build an opulent structure made out of purple amethyst marble. The

plan was rejected. This was a declaration of Every City's resolve to not be bribed by foreign interests. The first proposal for the Purple Tower also misunderstood the city's determination to modernise. Luxurious buildings with fanciful materials reminded the corruption of the old regime. What was needed was a far more spartan monument to celebrate the hard working citizens of the Old Boneyard. Even though a completely different design was finally built, it was decided that the monument will be called "Purple Tower" to remind everyone that Every City will write it's own destiny. I try to imagine this history as the waiter brings the instant coffee which I immediately regret ordering. Here we are sitting on top of a steel knot that was built on the whim of a tinpot dictator to celebrate modernising and there isn't even an espresso machine.

COFFEE IN EVERY CITY

Although coffee service is woefully inadequate and outrageously expensive at tourist attractions, Every City is by no means outside of the loop when it comes to the global third wave coffee revolution. The Old Boneyard is absolutely teeming with fancy coffee houses that serve their brews in sophisticated glassware straight out of a Chemistry lab. If you want to stick to familiar tastes, Every City is one of the cities with the largest number of **Queequeg** coffee chains in the world. So, no matter where you are in central Boneyard, you are never more than a stone's throw away from an extra large pumpkin latte with triple cream and caramel!

THE OLD BONEYARD

THE OLD BONEYARD

Homsin doesn't seem to mind his own coffee. His name has become almost synonymous with Every City. His popularity increased tremendously after receiving an international prize for literature. Every guidebook or journalistic account which offers an insiders view of the city queue up to get an inspiring quote from him. Homsin's books are renown for their descriptions of the City as a place overflowing with a collective sense of melancholy. He uses the local word *nüzüh*, to describe this sentiment. It is true that Every City is caught in the throes of an acute nostalgia. The afternoon sky reflects the famous silhouette of the city in a sepia tone, which contrasts starkly with the blue sea. The scenery is almost like a metaphor for the duality which encapsulates the city's melancholic spirit. This feeling is aggravated by a historic pulse. What makes Every City unique is that it has seen countless periods of rise and fall, and like a boat standing precariously on the crest of a giant wave it has stayed afloat.

A stone's throw away, I meet Eara at the *Grasslands*, the hip underground vegan cafe which she owns. She begs to differ from the dissident author's opinion: *nüzüh?* She asks, pouting her lips. "I don't know, maybe it's to do with age". To her, Every City is an exciting place full of opportunities. Both Eara and Homsin are representative of hopsters from different generations. Hopsters, are of course a staple feature of Every City. "Hopster" is an apt name, it describes how they leap from trend to trend at great speeds. This is not only a metaphor for how quickly they change their opinions and tastes but also how they literally lunge into the air to commute between trend nodes. Their lifestyle reflects on their appearance,

THE OLD BONEYARD

Their hind legs are disproportionately large and well muscled. These hind legs are also covered with a zigzagging exoskeleton, which is crucial for hopster mating rituals. Their lust for fashion leaves a remarkable impact on the environment of Every City. Every once in a while, a new trend will be so appetising that these otherwise free-spirited visionaries will form epic swarms that ravage entire neighbourhoods.

Eara is fully aware of her kind's occasional tendency for destruction. This is why she is a keen political activist. "I want to live in a world which is more free," she says passionately. Eara has a unique take on the burning issues of our time. She has a very lyrical way of asserting self-evident truths like: "we need diversity, not division." Her words re-affirms my faith that there is no problem in the world that can not be solved by love and intensive creative effort.

It is her open-minded and candid attitude which makes Grasslands such a popular place with hopsters from all over the world. The spiritual bond between the patrons in this environment is almost tangible. The sense of communion is of course strengthened by the deliciousness of the food. Eara's ethics is reflected all over the menu. "Our ingredients are completely organic", she declares, beaming with pride. We clasp our mandibles around an exceptionally chewy and delicious fern leaf. Eara informs me that she took traditional recipes and adapted them to international tastes, which is all the better because food around here tends to be notoriously spicy. This form of culinary experimentation by taking local recipes and making them more palatable to visitors is all the rage in Every City. And I can testify that it is working!

FOOD IN EVERY CITY

In the olden days, Every City served as a crucial cross-road on the Eastern spice roads. A glimpse into the kitchen of an ordinary inhabitant of Every City is like stepping into a rainbow of fragrance. This carnival of flavour however, might not always be suitable for the digestive system of visitors. When visiting Every City, it is important to remember that you don't need to feel pressured to enjoy or even try everything. The good news for travellers who have a sweet tooth is that you can indulge yourself in local delicacies like the **Plittipoo**. Do not be fooled by the unappetising name, these almond flavoured lentil-flour crepes filled with a range of fruits and condiments are absolutely delicious. What is more, they are completely vegan and gluten free!

After dining like the natives, Eara takes me around town to sample the irresistible nightlife of Every City. We start out at *Hush*, a mellow bar fashioned like a 1920's speakeasy. Even though the concept is imported, it fits the context of Every City surprisingly well and feels completely authentic. Although it is perfectly legal, alcohol consumption in public is traditionally frowned upon. Everything you do in Every City feels like it is tinged with danger, just enough to tickle your senses but not crush them.

An emerging trend in history writing points out

how these cosmopolitan trends rose to prominence in different cities during the first quarter of 20th century. This environment of cultural sophistication was beaten back by a rising tide of nationalism. But it is being rediscovered by foreign historians like Kayleigh Blanchette. In her groundbreaking work *Hopping Along: The Rise and Fall of the Jazz Age in Every City,* Blanchette takes the reader on a proverbial roller coaster through forgotten aspects of Every City's history. I explain to Eara that Jazz music was played in ballrooms all over the city, she feigns a courteous smile and averts her eyes. Visibly intimidated by the fact that I know her city better than she does. I am left to wonder if Every City will ever catch up with her former glory again. Thankfully, a new generation of adventurous backpackers with tangled dreadlocks are pouring in with their didgeridoos and their hank drums.

THE OLD BONEYARD

THE OLD BONEYARD

These young artists are the lifeline of Every City to the global musical culture.

Steve, a regular at *Hush*, is one such artist. His voice is very reassuring: "dude", he declares, "hospitality here is amazing!" Steve was a struggling artist back home and moved to Every City to jumpstart his career. He straddled about for a while giving language lessons to residents who are desperate to make a connection with the outside world. "Earning foreign currency helps" he declares, hardly concealing a cheeky wink. Now he DJs at a nightclub called *The Cave* once a week, where he mixes traditional spiritual music of Every City with heavy bass and electronic tracks. Conservative circles have already voiced concern over his appropriation of religion, but to Steve, that just means he is on the right track. He will also be having his first solo art exhibition soon "It's sort of like about everything that inspires me about this city, yeah?" Eara wants to get moving, the night is young. She's also tired of Steve talking about himself incessantly.

MUSIC IN EVERY CITY

Music has a very long history in Every City. The musical traditions of the people and the educated elite in the city have been diametrically opposed to each other since the Middle Ages. Back in those days, the folkloric tradition was much richer and more open to cross pollinating with foreign cultures, the elites on the other hand were stuck in palaces and temples to recite devotional poems. These poems were occasionally accompanied with a handful of instruments "authorised" by religious officials for being appropriate to the solemnity of religious service. Nowadays these positions seem to be reversed. The music scene among the city's young and vibrant hopsters is bursting with creative energy and excitement, with international bands and DJs reliably appearing in the city's respectable night life venues. The common people who have inherited a rich folkloric tradition however, seem to have dug themselves into a rut. Taxi cabs and tea gardens that service working class families blast a type of music called **Fodo**. These are largely Weepy tunes with repetitive melodies that encourage listeners to dutifully resign to their fate and abide all misfortune. Predictably, this does not exactly make for a very innovative musical experience.

We arrive at *Aquarium*, one of the most exciting spots in town for the professional young adults who work in the vibrant creative industries of Every City. Although mainly catering for the young and the hip, the doors of the *Aquarium* are wide open for everyone who can pay a small fortune for a cocktail. I can assure you they are well worth the price. Many of the cocktails are unique

THE OLD BONEYARD

THE OLD BONEYARD

combinations and some of them involve the local carda-mon flavoured spirit called *Yallah.* Ironically, the word also has a crucial place in the local religious tradition, it means 'path to enlightenment'. You will see locals slurp it down with great enthusiasm in many places, I will say that enlightenment must be an acquired taste and leave it at that.

There are booths of various sizes at the *Aquarium,* these are mainly occupied by business executives from The Hive who come down to impress their partners, not just with their money but also their patronage of cutting edge urban culture. The faint humming sound around these booths is audible, even with the pounding music. "Buzzies" Eara shouts in my ear "what do they know about partying?" The place is starting to warm up, there is a tangible quality to the sexual energy in the air. "How do hopsters party around here?" I ask her. She points to the dance floor to show a familiar sight of a young male hopster, wooing women around him by scraping his arms and legs, producing a creaking sound. His cadences and melodies are first grade and in perfect sync with the trendy music blasted by the DJ. Youngsters in Every City are indeed extremely style conscious. I notice a young woman on the edge of the platform respond to the male's signalling, her antennae straighten up with a sudden jerk. The male notices her interest and approaches in a slow but determined stride. I watch with amazement, this courting ritual could have been happening in any other major metropolis.

I hobble out of the nightclub, my head spinning from the libations. Fortunately, my hotel is nearby. *Ho-*

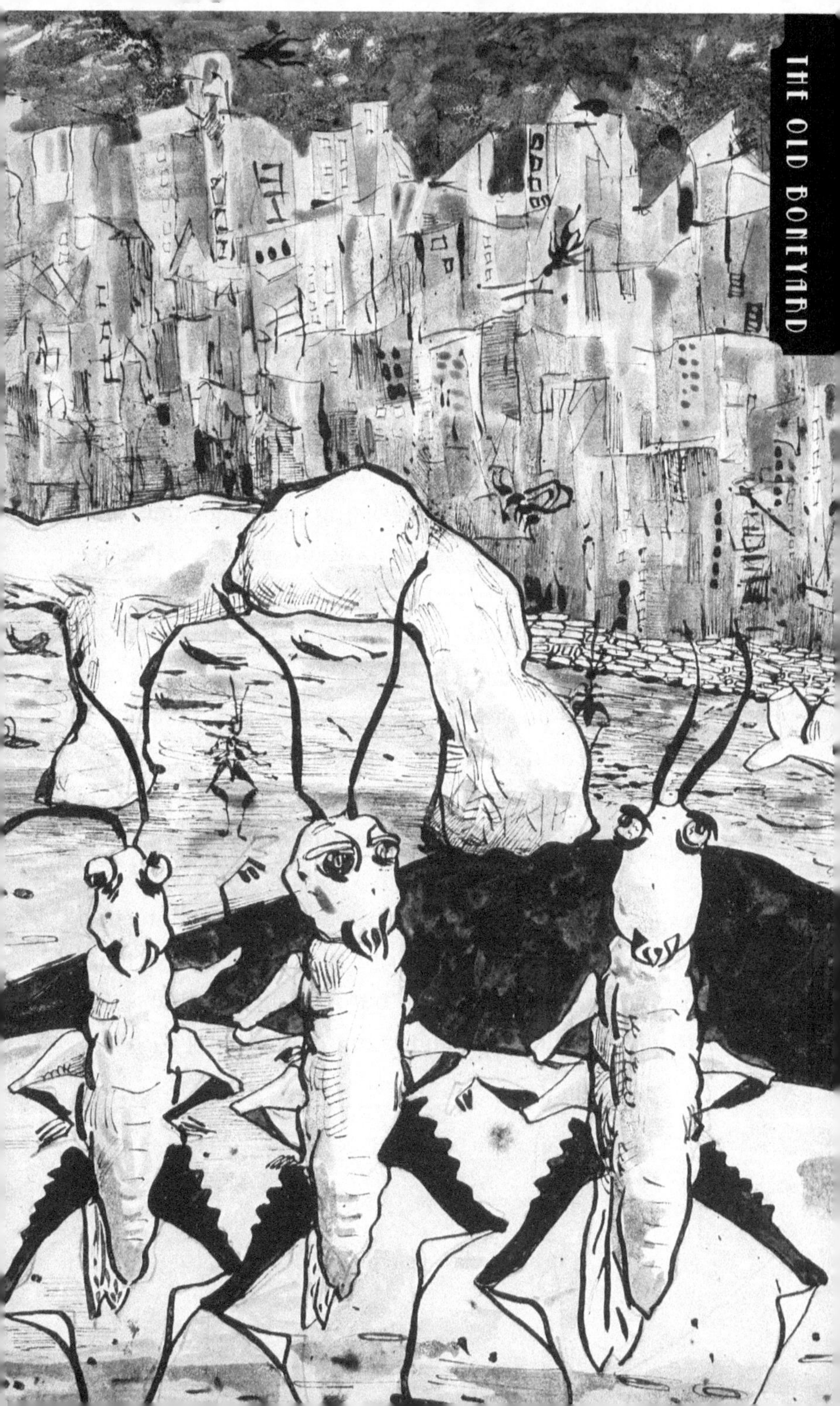
THE OLD BONEYARD

tel Xanadu is one of the hidden gems of the city, it sits firmly at a mid-price range and has all the basic creature comforts you would expect. The location reflects the competitive price. If you will be staying here, I would suggest taking a cab back at night. Although technically still in the Old Boneyard, it is literally at the border with Almond Valley. If you take a wrong turn you might suddenly find yourself in a completely different place. The ancient narrow streets lure the traveller like a labyrinth, frozen in time. I would recommend resisting the temptation until daytime, Almond Valley is not as accustomed to outsiders.

As I lay my head to rest, I can't help but compare the Every City of Maji Homsin to that of Eara. I have only spent a day in this city so far, yet it has been enough for me to discern that the defining feature of Every City is contrast. Homsin's eye sees the fountains and palaces of the city's golden age, sitting next to dusty construction sites and impoverished streets vendors. The scenery invites melancholy like an open wound invites infection. To Eara, Every City is an iridescent centre of activity. Her world has long crawled out from its dead husk and is leaping confidently into the future, pulsating with life.

—— • ——

HOTELS IN EVERY CITY

The rise of the hospitality industry in Every City dates back to the Cocaine Wars in early 19th Century, when a dispute with foreign dignitaries about the importation of narcotics into the country erupted in a series of skirmishes which culminated with the entry of expeditionary forces into the city. Prior to this incident, foreigners were only allowed to enter the city with a special permission granted by the royal court. These visitors would often have to improvise their accommodation through personal contacts and acquaintances. The Cocaine Wars brought along a rush of investment and a great number of high quality grand hotels began to appear all over the city. The first and most famous of these is **The Imperial**. Founded by the cocaine millionaire Maximus Whiteley during the heydays of global commerce, The Imperial still sets the standard for hotels across the world. It's vast ballroom has hosted countless heads of state and the most illustrious musical orchestras. Staying in this hotel is naturally outside the price range of most backpackers, but it is worth a visit just to soak in the atmosphere of it's grand lobby. Today the city is home to hundreds of hotels in an extremely wide price-range. For the lower end of the spectrum you can try the **Nimbus Mansions** a modern apartment complex of grey concrete built with the intention of providing cheap housing for the city's growing working class. Some of the residents have bought up multiple rooms to rent them out for visitors. The place is notorious for it's cramped rooms, do not expect to swing any cats in here. Also don't be surprised to see shady dealings in the corridors, Nimbus Mansions is something of a supermarket for all sorts of illicit goods (though of course you haven't heard that from this guide).

ALMOND

VALLEY

There are still plenty in Every City who carry the past on their shoulders like a giant shell. Unlike the hopsters in the Old Boneyard, they don't spring around weightlessly. The *sloggers* of Almond City, crawl at a slow and steady pace leaving a trace behind them. Sloggers are known for leaving a slimy substance on all types of surfaces that they drag their mucous body over. While sloggers are universally inclined to follow in each others' trails, here in Every City this behaviour is coded into spiritual texts.

In fact, their entire philosophy revolves around leaving traces and following them. Remember those cardamon flavoured drinks they were having at the *Aquarium*? Well, it turns out that *Yallah*, or "path to enlightenment", consists of following the traces of those who came before. I would go as far as to say that the key to understanding Every City is to understand *Yallah*. Each day you can see the great masses of sloggers whirling purposefully around Every City, with an expression of eternal contentment. You may think that *Yallah* is an exceptionally conservative idea, which stifles the kind of creativity that makes progress possible and perhaps, you may be right. For me, all I know is that if you drink enough glasses from the alcoholic beverage with the same name, you will get a unique insight into the virtues of whirling. The fact that *Yallah* can mean one thing in the Old Boneyard and something entirely different in Almond Valley, is a testimony to this civilisation's brilliant sense of humour.

It is now time to explore something that is *authentically* Every City. I want to dive straight into the heart of this place and solve its ancient secrets. The Old Boneyard has a vibrant cultural life and an exciting nightlife. But these attributes belong distinctly in the modern world and they have become universal among all major cities. To really get to the heart of Every City's enigma, I must discover it's ancient history. Unlike where I come from, in Every City, religion still plays a crucial role in everyday life. I have to admit before I came to Every City I had some preconceptions about religion and those who practice it. But here, I was struck with awe by the hospitality of residents. Everywhere I walked into, I was offered tea and coffee by hosts who never once asked for payment in return. This magical and abundant generosity convinced me of the power of travelling once again. With every sip of free tea, I felt myself shedding my preconceptions; until I felt so enlightened that I could literally acknowledge the validity of opinions and beliefs that were not identical to mine.

HOSPITALITY IN EVERY CITY

Regaling guests with a vast variety of treats is a timeless tradition in Every City that is almost considered an art form. Every household without exception, follows a long and sophisticated list of unspoken rules that govern how guests are to be fed and what subjects will be talked about. For example visits are categorised according to the significance of the occasion. A **kalaam** which literally means "short-sit" is when you stop by a friend or a relative at their home or their office to catch up. A kalaam can last anything from fifteen minutes to several hours and it usually either involves tea or a chosen alcoholic beverage, appropriate snacks are chosen according to the drink of choice. A "long-sit", known as a **salaam** is more like a dinner party. For a visit to qualify as a salaam there has to be more than two people present and at least three hot dishes have to be served. There are also certain rules that guests must be mindful of. Leaving your teaspoon inside the cup while drinking declares your intention to urinate on your hosts grave. If you find your plate being perpetually piled up far beyond your capacity to eat, it could be because you are scratching your nose. A gesture which means you are hungry. Although the last recorded incident of the examples above date back to the late 1600's it is still better to be safe than sorry.

Accompanying me on my journey are Abou and Mimi. Abou and Mimi are a young slogger couple who live in Almond Valley. Like many sloggers, they are resoundingly working class. We meet at a café overlooking the Main Temple. The interior decor reflects the combination of tradition and modernity which typifies Every City. Rattan furniture gives the sun-baked lobby area the light and airy feeling it desperately needs. Make no mistake this place is hot and humid in the summer.

I immediately ask them what they make of Yallah's dual meaning. They smile sheepishly, avoiding the question. Instead, Mimi, who has a surprisingly philosophical inclination, takes my inquiry as an opportunity to give a lecture on the virtues of her faith. Unfortunately for her, I already had too much Yallah the night before to be

lectured about the finer points of this obscure theological system. I interrupt her to re-iterate my question. They explain, almost apologetically that they don't drink. I sense a tickling sensation deep in my belly. It must be the smug satisfaction of knowing that I learned more about *Yallah* in one night than Abou and Mimi, who have devoted their lives to studying it. After finishing our coffee we stroll across the road to the Main Temple.

It is literally a drag to go anywhere with the sloggers of Almond Valley. I observe their giant molluscs bobbing up and down. Although they have antennae of their own, they serve a completely different purpose to the hopster antennae. While hopsters sense the world to sniff out novelty from miles away and leap great distances; all sloggers are interested in, is perceiving their immediate environment and calculating the most well-trodden path, so they don't stray too far off. In many ways, Abou and Mimi remind me of my own ma and pa, who are currently enjoying a quiet retirement after a lifetime of toil and reading the *Conservative Paper*. Future prospects for sloggers in Almond Valley may not be as bright as my parents, life expectancy is lower here. As if that wasn't bad enough the molluscs on Abou and Mimi's back are twice as big as my parents'. Despite the added weight, they plough along heroically.

Of course, in many ways, my parents wouldn't recognise anything of themselves in Abou and Mimi. Although sloggers' abdominal mucus is exactly the same substance everywhere and they all crawl around at the same frustrating pace, they still exhibit a great deal of variation in appearance, depending on geographic origin.

The average slogger in Every city is just a shade darker, their molluscs are slightly larger and patterned differently. Among the sapient species of our planet, the sloggers are the only ones who exhibit a significant diversity in appearance. It is almost impossible to look at a buzzie or a hopster and immediately determine where they come from. Even though these differences appear to be minor, they can make a huge difference, especially to other sloggers. The characteristic conservatism of sloggers makes them more likely to embrace bigoted ideologies. Buzzies have evolved out of their prejudice because their insatiable greed forces them into contact with other species; whereas hopsters (even those with a slogger background) are by nature open-minded and thus averse to prejudice.

After what seems like an eternity of crawling, we finally arrive at the temple. It is magnificent! just as I imagined it. The interior is vast and quiet. I feel a deep sense of communion with the place. The air you breathe within these walls is thick with centuries of civilisation. The gravity of history contrasts with the feeling of weightlessness I experience under the giant dome of the temple. The way Every City keeps throwing contrast after contrast with such unrelenting consistency, is almost surreal. I can't help but think that this city has been built specifically for travel writers to narrate ostentatious metaphors.

My reveries are interrupted by Abou who points to the marvellous wall decorations of the temple. He informs me that the intricate circular patterns on the hexagonal tiles are a direct reference to the spiritual philosophy of *Yallah.* His comfortable voice alerts me to my own stiffness. For many sloggers, temples like this one serve not just as places of worship but also places of public gathering. For some reason, I had simply assumed that it would be forbidden to speak in this sacred place. As I listen to Abou and Mimi telling me about the history of the temple, I realise that my dogged religious reverence may be overdone. It is often difficult for outsiders to know how to navigate a place like Almond Valley, the ease with

which the locals themselves go about their daily business only aggravates my own sense of anxiety. Almond Valley stretches over the history of civilisation like a tightrope. A moment of flippant irreverence can raise as many eyebrows as an excessive display of sincerity. The secrets of Every City are slippery. Each time I feel I have finally grasped them, they escape my grasp and disappear off my sight.

MAIN TEMPLE

The Main Temple was built in six hundred *Before the Great Saviour* as a Pantheon for all the gods of Every City. But when **King Kyarduc the Grim** came to power eighteen hundred years later, he founded Truitry and famously declared it "the one True religion". Kyraduc's reputation for Grimness is well deserved, his religious teachings place a singular emphasis on asceticism and sense of duty. The more sensual and hedonistic aspects of Truidic culture that we came to know through writers like Jean Lozé (discussed below) were gradually introduced into the religion by a succession of rulers, priests and artists. This entire history has manifested itself on the interior decorations of the temple. Historical sources indicate that the original Pantheon housed very large statues of the seven gods. The interior of the dome was decorated with frescos that depicted ancient ritual dances and animal sacrifices. Kyraduc ordered the statues to be removed and earned a great deal of diplomatic points by gifting them to foreign rulers he wanted to be on friendly terms with. He later covered the frescos with a plaster, to be hidden for centuries. Over time this new blank surface became home for some of the finest artists from the Truitrian tradition and was covered with intricate and beautiful designs. This period also did not last forever. As the winds of modernisation swept the world, Every City started to go through some major changes. The modernising dictator who built the Purple Tower decided that religion was holding Every City back from reaching the level of advanced civilisations. The plaster that covered the dome was carefully peeled off to reveal the original artwork. The Temple still serves as a museum today accommodating hundreds of tourists every day. Unfortunately the current populist government has intentions to convert the Main Temple into a place of worship once again. A move which raises an uncomfortable question: will Every City *ever* reach the level of advanced civilisations?

ALMOND VALLEY

ALMOND VALLEY

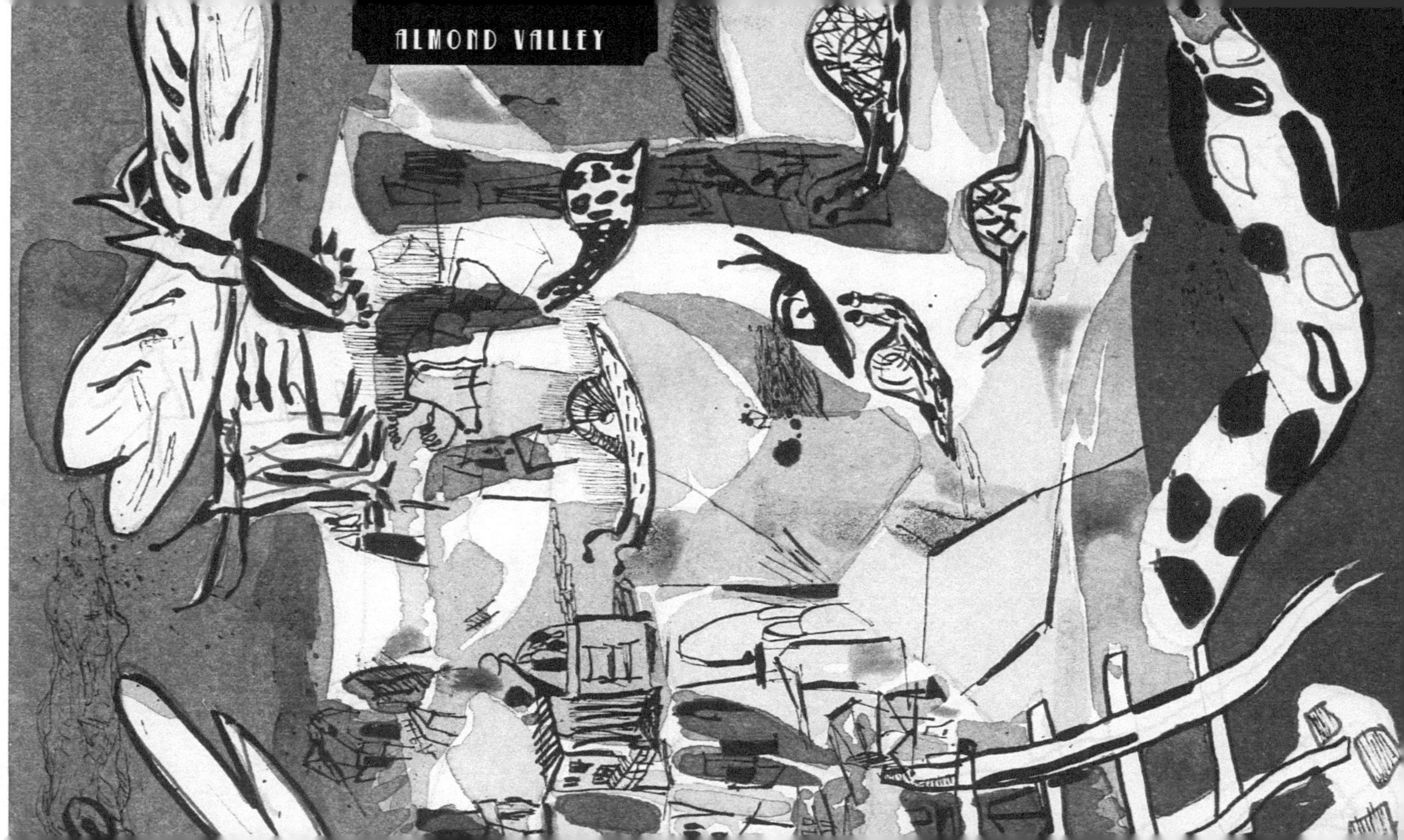
ALMOND VALLEY

I am not the first to be intoxicated by the secrets of this enigmatic city. Generations of writers and poets who visited Every City have been enamoured by its mystique. As the city is experiencing a contemporary Renaissance, the sense of mystery remains. The introduction of modernity over the last century has made the place even more mysterious. Of all the writers who have been here, none captures the sense of mystery like the legendary poet and sailor Jean Lozé. Lozé was a familiar face in Every City during a period of very rapid changes. His poetry is filled with eulogies to the city's authentic spirit. Lozé mourned what he saw as the forced introduction of modernity into his misty narrow labyrinths of cobblestone. These charming vestiges of a romantic era are now replaced by busy motorised highways. Against this destruction, Lozé grieved as if he had lost a lover.

Although Every City has changed a lot since the days of Lozé, it is impossible to not remember his words:

Mournful kingdom of turquoise
Fill me with your delicious dread
I yearn to be under your marble dome
Eternally blessed by your haze
As your memory fades, like sand dunes
I yearn to vanish in your salt seas

Many in Almond Valley only know Lozé's name from a scenic spot overlooking Every City named after him. There is something slightly disappointing about the disappearance of a character like Lozé from the public memory of Every City. This is the man whose literary genius has helped bring Every City to global public attention.

The period of mutations observed by Lozé has come to its conclusion, and the poet's romantic vision of the city is a clear loser. The story of Every City's modernisation is not such a black and white affair for my hosts. "Of course we have lost a lot of our identity during modernisation" starts Abou, leaving Mimi to complete his sentence: "but it was also necessary." They tell me about changes in the economy, about the infrastructure projects that are necessary to sustain a giant metropolis like Every City. This is all well and good, but what attracted me and Lozé to this city is not plumbing and transportation, but rather a profound sense of mystery and wonder.

I was hoping Abou and Mimi would be my guides through the maze of Every City's soul, my sherpas on the uphill journey to the misty peak of the city's complicated spirituality. But instead, I find them calculating the costs of raising offsprings or computing the optimal route for their frequent commutes. I would not have imagined the residents of this wondrous city to be so bereft of spiritual depth. I can't decide if I am more disappointed by the apathy I am witnessing or by all the poets who have misguided my expectations. Regardless, the architectural wonders I laid eyes on today are immensely impressive in their own right. A wholly different journey awaits me tomorrow. I will venture into the Hive and witness the throbbing heart of Every City. This is the place where decisions are made. A hub of activity on which thousands rush around with a tremendous sense of purpose.

—— • ——

THE

HIVE

Once again, I am fortunate to have a local guide. Muzra's family have been living in the Hive for eight generations. Foreign-educated and eloquent, he has the habit of frequently rubbing his hands like all buzzies. He greets me with a cordial smile and immediately asks me what school I went to. He winces when I reply, clearly not impressed. For a young buzzie like Muzra, receiving an education in prestigious international schools is a point of pride. Young buzzies are particularly keen on competing about their education, Muzra is no exception.

Aside from their wings, the most significant anatomical feature of buzzies is their eyes. Each buzzie eye contains hundreds of tiny lenses. The mind of a buzzie is like a CCTV control room with hundreds of screens. This particular anatomical feature comes with its pros and cons. Buzzie eyes excel in detecting motion because objects emerge and fade from multiple lenses. However, they miss out on perceiving colour and texture. Flying at great speeds is one of the crucial aspects of buzzies' life. This is why it is essential for them, to spot sudden movements and react instantly. This anatomic attribute makes buzzies very adept at spotting both danger and oppor-

tunity before anyone else. But evolution is a zero-sum game. For buzzies, this means their extraordinary motion sensors come at the cost of not being able to fully appreciate the afternoon sunset, or the change of colours each season. While it is certainly easy to feel contempt for them, it is worth remembering that they are deprived of the pleasures we take for granted.

Buzzies and hopsters have always had a tense relationship. Since the dawn of time, hopsters like me have relied on the support of buzzies like Muzra for patronage and financial support. But on the other hand, buzzies have traditionally usurped the creative energy of hopsters and turned it into business investments or political propaganda. As I am reflecting on this fundamental divide between us, he rapidly ushers me into a Queequeg coffee store. We are back out almost as soon as we got in, clutching our cardboard to-go cups. Having to wait

THE HIVE

THE HIVE

for Abou and Mimi to catch up with me seems like a distant and pleasant memory. I try to strike a conversation with small platitudes. Muzra nods briskly the first few times. When I tell him something along the lines of "wow! Things work so fast here", he responds abruptly "what did you expect?"

I quickly realise that the historic dynamics underneath our mutual lack of chemistry is more complex than I first thought. Beyond the usual buzziehopster tension, Muzra and I are also having a culture clash, due to our geographic origins. Dissecting the politics of a buzzie is never easy. They are not quite like sloggers, whose sense of attachment with the land is literally reflected in the anatomy of their locomotion. They are not like hopsters, who are simply incapable of belonging to any particular place or time. Buzzies derive both their politics and their sense of identity from one thing alone: greed. Although the recent economic rise of Every City is providing Muzra plenty of opportunities, many local buzzies can not shake the memory of their domination by other nations. To fully understand Muzra's feelings, we must first look at the nature of buzzies, then focus on specific turning points in Every City's history.

COCAINE WARS

Following the Cocaine wars of early 19th century, the city was ruled by a puppet king who was placed on the throne by the occupying forces of the **Seven-Nation Consortium.** This period is remembered by the residents of Every City as "kinda-feudal, kinda-colonised." Although official historians of Every City are not exactly fond of this period, it is a time for tremendous development. The city's first railway and telegraph lines was built by foreign investors. The first modern hospital in the city was built by the Horace Kingsley foundation. Kingsley is a household name across the world as the founder of Regular Oil & Co and for being the epitome of monopolistic capitalism. But sadly, little is remembered of the great work the Kingsley family have done all over the world through their philanthropic institutions. Of course, the Seven-Nation Consortium was not always fair in it's treatment of the natives. Widespread addiction to cocaine during this period is still remembered for being profoundly damaging to national pride. The emotional scars from this period run deep and continue to poison the natives' relationship with the outside world. Acclaimed Every City historian Fred Döttkeir's recent contribution to this debate *Myth of the Cocaine Plague,* tears through the emotional mist that clouds judgements on the issue of Cocaine Wars.

Most outsiders look at the world of buzzies and see a well-oiled machine guided by expertly calculated interests. But behind the curtains; the grey army of bankers, lawyers and politicians are all trampling over each other to get a bigger slice. The psychology of buzzies is as cu-

THE HIVE

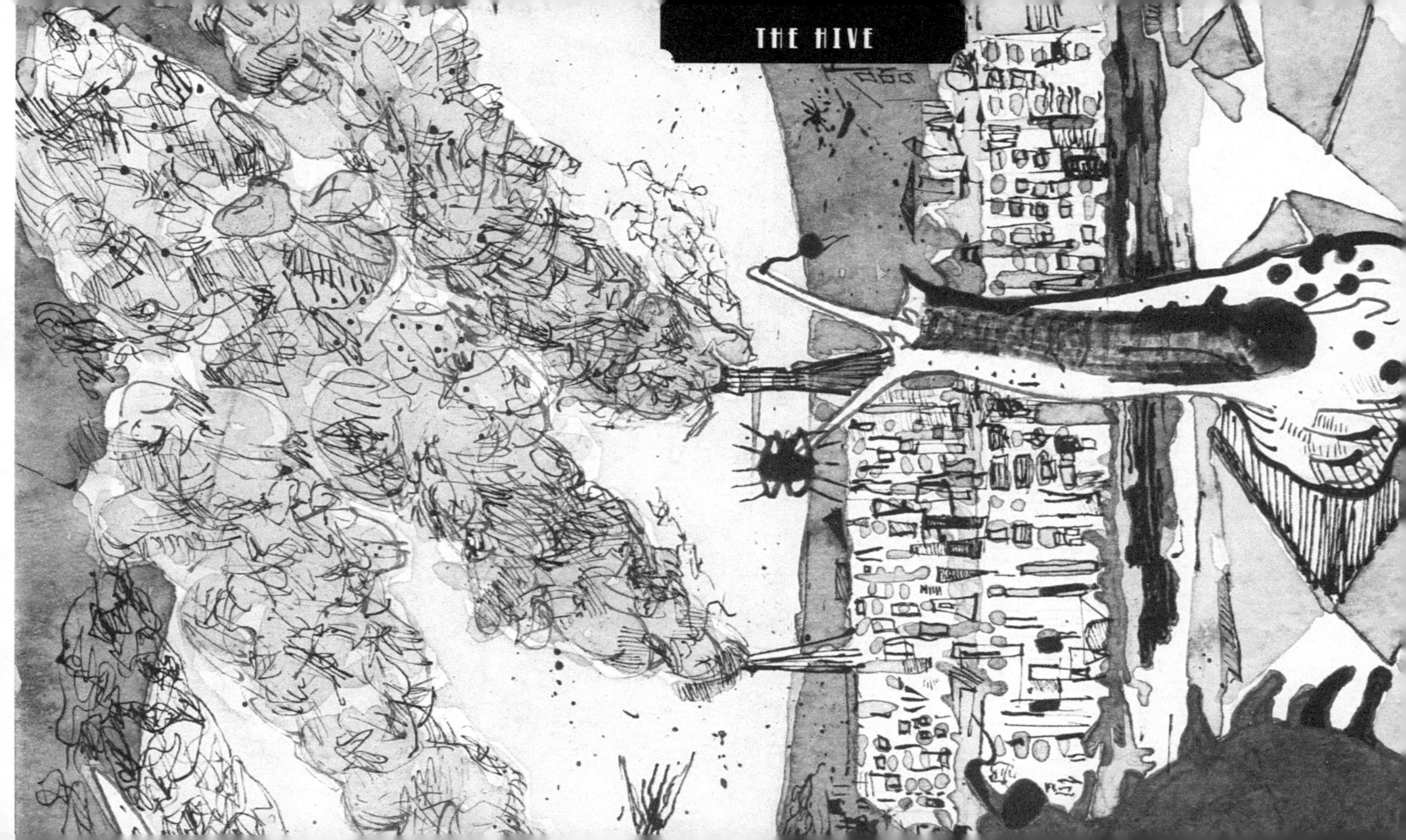
THE HIVE

rious as the nature of capitalism. On the surface, every buzzie is ill-at-ease in the company of ideologies which make strong appeals to emotions. But they also know that manipulating the feelings of others, is one of the most guaranteed ways of making big money. There have been historic moments in which buzzies have lost their grip on power, due to large upheavals or internal rivalry. In these turning points, they have adapted to prevailing ideas and managed to come out on top in the long run.

Business districts like the Hive have always been fascinating to me. As we rush through the swarm of grey suits, I imagine what this place must look like on the weekends. I am mesmerised by how financial districts are always deserted during off hours. By night time, everyone here will recede like the tide. Nothing will remain of them except for the remnants of their ready-made-workinglunches: discarded cardboard sandwich boxes with plastic windows, instant noodle cups and pocket size aluminium sauce bags shrivelled after being extracted with excessive precision.

Muzra unexpectedly starts to recite an entirely unsolicited lecture on history. His lecture starts from the collapse of the old monarchy at the dawn of the last century. It seems the great empire has collapsed because of inner corruption and ominous "foreign meddling". Next chapter in this official history is "the Great Revolutionary War." Muzra's attachment to this version of history is predictable. The corrupt absolute monarchy was abolished, imperialists were kicked out and a process of modernisation was initiated.

This version of events is remarkably popular in Every City. I understand that it has been a necessary founding myth for citizens. But to me, as a citizen of the so-called "imperialist" countries, it makes me feel deeply uncomfortable. I feel like confronting Muzra by telling him that it was us who have laid the infrastructure for *their* modernisation. It was us who have built the railroads and the telegraph lines that have enabled *their* great leap into modernity. But I just don't have it in me to start what promises to be a very fruitless argument. I would much rather appreciate my present environment.

I ponder leisurely on this history as we reach the Seat of Government. Every trip to the Hive has to start with this complex of buildings. This is the spot where consecutive forms of governance have passed the torch to each other in what seems like five hundred years of miraculous continuity. The place was first built in the 1560s as a walled compound. For a long time, it was called a "city within a city" by the locals. Far more than a simple abode for the ruler and his many concubines, the Seat of Government also housed the offices of top bureaucrats who were charged with informing their ruler. The complex is designed as a selfsufficient settlement with a wide range of services. Rulers of every city had a personal barber, tailor and even a confectionery, presumably for late night snacks after a busy day of ruling the nation. Aside from amenities, the city within the city also had dwellings for artists, composers and poets.

Muzra has a peculiar sense of hospitality. He glides at light speed, drawing a figure eight across the floor, pointing to this object or that work of art. I appreciate

THE HIVE

THE HIVE

his enthusiasm, but can't help but feel like he is trying to dictate my experience of Every City. My aversion to authority makes it really difficult to enjoy his hospitality. I notice his exuberance wane as soon as we walk out of the Seat of Government. We briskly shake hands and depart as unexpectedly as we have met.

My long-weekend break is coming to a close and there is nothing I would like more than to stretch my legs and digest the experience. Thankfully, this is exactly what Reginald Mansfield III suggests we do when he invites me for cocktails on the terrace bar of *Hotel Elegance*. Reginald is what is known colloquially as an "old hand." He has been living and conducting business in Every city for over twenty-five years. He is often unofficially consulted by his government about his opinion on Every City. He is alarmed about the new generation of Foreign Service officers who are getting more and more gung-ho. "You can get much further here by being gentle." He mutters pensively.

I tell him about my day with Muzra and his own belligerent version of history. He slaps the air back and forth as if to say "I have heard it all before". Indeed, the-peaceful world we inherited from buzzies like Reginald is collapsing. Polarisation and hostility are once again on the rise. Every City is a unique place to observe the fractures that run through our modern world. We toast champagne from slender glasses and gulp it down. "The one problem with living here..." Reginald muses merrily "is the variation in the quality of champagne." I whirl my own glass like it was a test tube and conclude "tastes a bit like a bubble bath." We both let out a hearty laugh.

From the terrace of *Elegance* All the finest monuments of the city are laid out in front of us. On one side is the Main Temple carrying the great weight of tradition. On the other side, the Purple Tower protrudes through the lethargy of history to remind us of Every City's determination for progress. We are too close to the Seat of government from our vantage point to see it clearly, but we can literally hear the intense traffic of buzzies. I feel like I have come full circle since my meeting with Homsin. Once again, I am standing high above the city overlooking an astounding silhouette. Despite some disappointments,experiencing Every City in three days has been an intense and thrilling experience. I will never be the same again.